Francis Frith's
Lake District

Photographic Memories

Francis Frith's
Lake District

Revised edition of original work by

Roly Smith

FRITH
BOOK Co

First published in the United Kingdom in 2001 by
The Francis Frith Collection

Paperback Edition 2001
ISBN 1-85937-275-9

Hardback Edition 2001
ISBN 1-85937-356-9

British Library Cataloguing in Publication Data

Francis Frith's Lake District
Roly Smith

The Francis Frith Collection
Frith's Barn, Teffont,
Salisbury, Wiltshire SP3 5QP
Tel: +44 (0) 1722 716 376
Email: info@francisfrith.co.uk
www.francisfrith.com

Printed and bound in Great Britain

Front Cover: Newby Bridge, the Swan Hotel 1914 67414p

The colour-tinting is for illustrative purposes only, and is not intended to be historically accurate

AS WITH ANY HISTORICAL DATABASE THE FRITH ARCHIVE IS CONSTANTLY BEING CORRECTED AND IMPROVED
AND THE PUBLISHERS WOULD WELCOME INFORMATION ON OMISSIONS OR INACCURACIES

Contents

Francis Frith: *Victorian Pioneer*

FRANCIS FRITH, Victorian founder of the world-famous photographic archive, was a complex and multi-talented man. A devout Quaker and a highly successful Victorian businessman, he was both philosophic by nature and pioneering in outlook.

By 1855 Francis Frith had already established a wholesale grocery business in Liverpool, and sold it for the astonishing sum of £200,000, which is the equivalent today of over £15,000,000. Now a multi-millionaire, he was able to indulge his passion for travel. As a child he had pored over travel books written by early explorers, and his fancy and imagination had been stirred by family holidays to the sublime mountain regions of Wales and Scotland. 'What a land of spirit-stirring and enriching scenes and places!' he had written. He was to return to these scenes of grandeur in later years to 'recapture the thousands of vivid and tender memories', but with a different purpose. Now in his thirties, and captivated by the new science of photography, Frith set out on a series of pioneering journeys to the Nile regions that occupied him from 1856 until 1860.

Intrigue and Adventure

He took with him on his travels a specially-designed wicker carriage that acted as both dark-room and sleeping chamber. These far-flung journeys were packed with intrigue and adventure. In his life story, written when he was sixty-three, Frith tells of being held captive by bandits, and of fighting 'an awful midnight battle to the very point of surrender with a deadly pack of hungry, wild dogs'. Sporting flowing Arab costume, Frith arrived at Akaba by camel seventy years before Lawrence, where he encountered 'desert princes and rival sheikhs, blazing with jewel-hilted swords'.

During these extraordinary adventures he was assiduously exploring the desert regions bordering the Nile and patiently recording the antiquities and peoples with his camera. He was the first photographer to venture beyond the sixth cataract. Africa was still the mysterious 'Dark Continent', and Stanley and Livingstone's historic meeting was a decade into the future. The conditions for picture taking confound belief. He laboured for hours in his wicker dark-room in the sweltering heat of the desert, while the volatile chemicals fizzed dangerously in their trays. Often he was forced to work in remote tombs and caves where conditions were cooler. Back in London he exhibited his photographs and was 'rapturously cheered' by members of the Royal Society. His reputation as a

photographer was made overnight. An eminent modern historian has likened their impact on the population of the time to that on our own generation of the first photographs taken on the surface of the moon.

Venture of a Life-Time

Characteristically, Frith quickly spotted the opportunity to create a new business as a specialist publisher of photographs. He lived in an era of immense and sometimes violent change. For the poor in the early part of Victoria's reign work was a drudge and the hours long, and people had precious little free time to enjoy themselves. Most had no transport other than a cart or gig at their disposal, and had not travelled far beyond the boundaries of their own town or village. However,

by the 1870s, the railways had threaded their way across the country, and Bank Holidays and half-day Saturdays had been made obligatory by Act of Parliament. All of a sudden the ordinary working man and his family were able to enjoy days out and see a little more of the world.

With characteristic business acumen, Francis Frith foresaw that these new tourists would enjoy having souvenirs to commemorate their days out. In 1860 he married Mary Ann Rosling and set out with the intention of photographing every city, town and village in Britain. For the next thirty years he travelled the country by train and by pony and trap, producing fine photographs of seaside resorts and beauty spots that were keenly bought by millions of Victorians. These prints were painstakingly pasted into family albums and pored over during the dark nights of winter, rekindling precious memories of summer excursions.

The Rise of Frith & Co

Frith's studio was soon supplying retail shops all over the country. To meet the demand he gathered about him a small team of photographers, and published the work of independent artist-photographers of the calibre of Roger Fenton and Francis Bedford. In order to gain some understanding of the scale of Frith's business one only has to look at the catalogue issued by Frith & Co in 1886: it runs to some 670 pages, listing not only many thousands of views of the British Isles but also many photographs of most European countries, and China, Japan, the USA and Canada — note the sample page shown above from the hand-written *Frith & Co* ledgers detailing pictures taken. By 1890 Frith had created the greatest specialist photographic publishing company in the world,

with over 2,000 outlets – more than the combined number that Boots and WH Smith have today! The picture on the right shows the *Frith & Co* display board at Ingleton in the Yorkshire Dales. Beautifully constructed with mahogany frame and gilt inserts, it could display up to a dozen local scenes.

Postcard Bonanza

The ever-popular holiday postcard we know today took many years to develop. In 1870 the Post Office issued the first plain cards, with a pre-printed stamp on one face. In 1894 they allowed other publishers' cards to be sent through the mail with an attached adhesive halfpenny stamp. Demand grew rapidly, and in 1895 a new size of postcard was permitted called the court card, but there was little room for illustration. In 1899, a year after

Frith's death, a new card measuring 5.5 x 3.5 inches became the standard format, but it was not until 1902 that the divided back came into being, with address and message on one face and a full-size illustration on the other. *Frith & Co* were in the vanguard of postcard development, and Frith's sons Eustace and Cyril continued their father's monumental task, expanding the number of views offered to the public and recording more and more places in Britain, as the coasts and countryside were opened up to mass travel.

Francis Frith died in 1898 at his villa in Cannes, his great project still growing. The archive he created continued in business for another seventy years. By 1970 it contained over a third of a million pictures of 7,000 cities, towns and villages. The massive photographic record Frith has left to us stands as a living monument to a special and very remarkable man.

Frith's Archive: *A Unique Legacy*

FRANCIS FRITH'S legacy to us today is of immense significance and value, for the magnificent archive of evocative photographs he created provides a unique record of change in 7,000 cities, towns and villages throughout Britain over a century and more. Frith and his fellow studio photographers revisited locations many times down the years to update their views, compiling for us an enthralling and colourful pageant of British life and character.

We tend to think of Frith's sepia views of Britain as nostalgic, for most of us use them to conjure up memories of places in our own lives with which we have family associations. It often makes us forget that to Francis Frith they were records of daily life as it was actually being lived in the cities, towns and villages of his day. The Victorian age was one of great and often bewildering change for ordinary people, and though the pictures evoke an

impression of slower times, life was as busy and hectic as it is today.

We are fortunate that Frith was a photographer of the people, dedicated to recording the minutiae of everyday life. For it is this sheer wealth of visual data, the painstaking chronicle of changes in dress, transport, street layouts, buildings, housing, engineering and landscape that captivates us so much today. His remarkable images offer us a powerful link with the past and with the lives of our ancestors.

Today's Technology

Computers have now made it possible for Frith's many thousands of images to be accessed almost instantly. In the Frith archive today, each photograph is carefully 'digitised' then stored on a CD Rom. Frith archivists can locate a single photograph amongst thousands within seconds. Views can be catalogued and sorted under a variety of categories of place and content to the immediate benefit of researchers.

Inexpensive reference prints can be created for them at the touch of a mouse button, and a wide range of books and other printed materials assembled and published for a wider, more general readership - in the next twelve months over a hundred Frith local history titles will be published! The day-to-day workings of the archive are very different from how they were in Francis Frith's time: imagine the herculean task of sorting through eleven tons of glass negatives as Frith had to do to locate a particular sequence of pictures! Yet

See Frith at www. frithbook.co.uk

the archive still prides itself on maintaining the same high standards of excellence laid down by Francis Frith, including the painstaking cataloguing and indexing of every view.

It is curious to reflect on how the internet now allows researchers in America and elsewhere greater instant access to the archive than Frith himself ever enjoyed. Many thousands of individual views can be called up on screen within seconds on one of the Frith internet sites, enabling people living continents away to revisit the streets of their ancestral home town, or view places in Britain where they have enjoyed holidays. Many overseas researchers welcome the chance to view special theme selections, such as transport, sports, costume and ancient monuments.

We are certain that Francis Frith would have heartily approved of these modern developments in imaging techniques, for he himself was always working at the very limits of Victorian photographic technology.

The Value of the Archive Today

Because of the benefits brought by the computer, Frith's images are increasingly studied by social historians, by researchers into genealogy and ancestory, by architects, town planners, and by teachers and schoolchildren involved in local history projects.

In addition, the archive offers every one of us an opportunity to examine the places where we and our families have lived and worked down the years. Highly successful in Frith's own era, the archive is now, a century and more on, entering a new phase of popularity.

The Past in Tune with the Future

Historians consider the Francis Frith Collection to be of prime national importance. It is the only archive of its kind remaining in private ownership and has been valued at a million pounds. However, this figure is now rapidly increasing as digital technology enables more and more people around the world to enjoy its benefits.

Francis Frith's archive is now housed in an historic timber barn in the beautiful village of Teffont in Wiltshire. Its founder would not recognize the archive office as it is today. In place of the many thousands of dusty boxes containing glass plate negatives and an all-pervading odour of photographic chemicals, there are now ranks of computer screens. He would be amazed to watch his images travelling round the world at unimaginable speeds through network and internet lines.

The archive's future is both bright and exciting. Francis Frith, with his unshakeable belief in making photographs available to the greatest number of people, would undoubtedly approve of what is being done today with his lifetime's work. His photographs, depicting our shared past, are now bringing pleasure and enlightenment to millions around the world a century and more after his death.

Villages

Most of the larger villages and towns of the Lake District occupy the most favoured sites in the valley bottoms, or command important river crossings. Although they may be small, many places have the urban air of small townships, which is exactly what they were in the days when the grant of a right to hold a market made the settlement, however tiny, an important trading centre for the surrounding countryside.

Newby Bridge, By the River 1914 67414
A family group of children enjoy a boating trip on the River Leven at Newby Bridge, at the southern end of Windermere. In the background is the 16th-century five-arched bridge which gave the village its name.

Troutbeck, General View c1880 12522
The name of this small settlement on the slopes of Wansfell Pike between Windermere and the Kirkstone Pass means exactly what it says - 'the trout stream' - and it stands above a stream with the same name. At the south end of the village is Townend, a typical Lakeland statesman's house, now in the care of the National Trust.

Troutbeck, The Valley c1880 12523
The Troutbeck valley is one of the quietest in the Lake District, and in this view, taken from the old coach route between Windermere and Penrith, the essentially rural nature of much of the district can still be appreciated. The white-painted farmhouse in the valley was probably occupied by one of the district's famous 'statesmen' farmers.

Eamont Bridge 1893 32934
Eamont Bridge, just south of Penrith on the A6, takes its name from this splendid three-arched bridge across the River Eamont. It is perhaps best known for its two prehistoric monuments: King Arthur's Round Table, a Bronze Age henge, and the former Neolithic stone circle and henge at Mayburgh, of which only one standing stone now remains.

Eamont Bridge, The Hotel 1893 32932
The proprietress of Taylforth's Hotel (left), in the main street of Eamont Bridge, stands outside to bid farewell to a guest departing in a pony and trap. The photographer would certainly not be able to set up his tripod in the middle of the same street today!

Coniston, The Parish Church 1929 82799
The blue-grey slate walls of Coniston parish church looks down on a memorial to one of England's greatest writers and social reformers, John Ruskin. He lived for nearly 30 years at Brantwood, opposite the village on the eastern shore of the lake, and preferred to be buried here, rather than to have a grander tomb in Westminster Abbey.

Coniston, From the Church Tower 1906 54242
This view from the church tower looks towards the wooded slopes of High Guards and up the valley of the Yewdale Beck. The whitewashed cottages of the village cluster around the church where the Yewdale Beck enters to the western side of Coniston Water.

Coniston, The Village 1929 82798
A pair of ramblers (right) heading for the hills stride out purposefully past the Rayburne Hotel and cafe in the centre of Coniston village. The lack of traffic in the main street is in sharp contrast with the scene today in this busy little village in the south-west Lakes.

▼ Ambleside, From Loughrigg 1892 30481
This general view of Ambleside, at the northern end of Windermere, was taken from the slopes of Loughrigg Fell. The spire of the parish church watches over this bustling village, which was founded in the 15th century; it once had thriving corn and bobbin mills on the River Rothay.

▼ Ambleside, From the Gate 1886 18672
We are looking down on the village centre from The Gate, facing the Rydal Fells. The fine Victorian buildings reflect the increased prosperity brought to the village by the tourist trade, which was just starting to burgeon at the time.

▲ Ambleside, The Queen's Hotel 1892
30484
The umbrellas on the coach-and-four drawn up outside the ornate frontage of the Queen's Hotel appear to have been raised to protect the holders from the sun, rather than the rain. Other coaches wait for their passengers outside the other hotels for a day on the lakes.

◀ **Ambleside, The Village 1912** 64305
Twenty years after photograph No 30484 was taken, the coach and horses in the centre of Ambleside have been replaced by open motor cars and charabancs.

Ambleside, The White Lion and Royal Oak Hotels 1912

64303

We are in the centre of Ambleside; Lamb's Royal Oak Hotel is on the left, and the White Lion Hotel is in the centre. A coach-and-four has pulled up outside the White Lion, while bustle in the main street shows how busy Ambleside had become as a tourist centre by this time.

Ambleside, Market Place 1927 79174
This photograph looks south from the Market Place. The street is almost deserted apart from a motor lorry, motorcycle and a few pedestrians, showing that the photograph was probably taken in the winter, outside the tourist season.

Ambleside, Bridge House 1912 64306
Easily the most famous and most photographed building in Ambleside is Bridge House, a tiny one-up, one-down house constructed on a bridge over the Stock Beck. Originally built in the 17th century as the apple-store for Ambleside Hall, it is now a National Trust Information Centre.

Grasmere, Red Lion Square 1926 79206
The Red Lion Hotel, on the right of the picture, gives its name to the square in the centre of the village, now dominated by traffic in a one-way system. The two cyclists meandering down the middle of the road would not be able to do so for long today!

Grasmere, The Church 1926 79209
The 13th-century parish church of St Oswald is now the centre of a hectic one-way traffic system. A rare annual rush-bearing ceremony is held at the church. Buried in the churchyard are William Wordsworth, his wife, Mary, his loving sister Dorothy, and the other members of the Wordsworth family.

Grasmere, Church Stile 1926 79208

Church Stile is the name of the road which goes around the parish church. Notice the charming cottage draped with creeper opposite the churchyard with its unusual porch, and the village shop next to it. The shopkeeper is advertising flowers and plants of all kinds, including ferns and alpines.

▼ **Grasmere, Wordsworth's Cottage 1936** 87636

William Wordsworth lived with his sister, Dorothy, at Dove Cottage, just outside the village, from 1799 to 1813. He wrote some of his best known poetry here. The cottage is now part of a museum dedicated to the life and work of the poet - the founder of the Lakeland Romantic Movement.

Grasmere, The Rothay Hotel 1912 64338

Horse-drawn coaches and a motor car are drawn up outside the Rothay Hotel. The fast-growing tourist trade made hotels such as this popular in the late 19th and early 20th centuries.

Hawkshead, From Charity High 1896 38820
Here we see the south Lakeland village from the hill of Charity High, just outside the village. Hawkshead is one of the prettiest Lakeland villages; it stands at the head of Esthwaite Water, and was probably founded in the 10th century by a Norseman called Haukr.

Hawkshead, The Parish Church 1892 30534
The parish church of St Michael is one of the most interesting in the Lake District. It was originally built as a chapel in the 12th century; the present commanding building on its hill overlooking the village mainly dates from the 15th century. It contains Tudor murals and painted texts on its walls, and its parish registers go back to the same period.

Hawkshead, The Bobbin Mill 1896 38836
Bobbin manufacture for the wool and cotton mills of the north of England was once an important industry in the well-wooded Lake District. Only 80 years ago, there were an estimated 25 bobbin mills similar to the one photographed here at Hawkshead still in production.

▲ Hawkshead, Market Square 1929 82372
A holidaying family relax with their dog outside the Old King's Arms pub and boarding house in the cobbled centre of the ancient village of Hawkshead. There have been a few changes here since the time of photograph No 38828: the gas lamp (left) has gone, the left-hand porch has been replaced, and the creeper on the centre porch seems to have migrated to the wall.

◄ Hawkshead, The Square 1896 38828
This picturesque cobbled square is in the centre of Hawkshead. An upended cart awaits its horse, while a little girl gazes across the empty square in anticipation. Now that most traffic by-passes this picturesque village, visitors can once again enjoy views like this, although it is seldom as quiet as here.

Hawkshead, The Village 1896 38831
The shops in the centre of Hawkshead are waiting for the tourists to arrive. The grey slate walls of the buildings and cobbled streets are typical of many Lakeland villages. On the wall alongside the door are display boards advertising *Frith & Co* local photographs.

Hawkshead, The Grammar School 1892 30538
William Wordsworth must have looked out from these mullioned windows of the ancient Grammar School, where he was educated between 1779 and 1787. The school, now a museum and library, sits comfortably beneath the bank on which the parish church of St Michael, seen in the background, stands.

Hawkshead, Flag Street 1892 30537

It is easy to see how this narrow Hawkshead street got its name, as it is paved by flagstones. The overhanging first-floor jetties of the whitewashed houses add to the medieval charm of the village, which is a favourite of the many visitors to the Lake District.

Windermere, Victoria Street 1929 82818
There is not much traffic to be seen in Victoria Street at this time. Victoria Street leads off Church Street, now the A591, in this busy little town; it was originally known as Birthwaite, but it changed its name to match that of the nearby lake when the railway arrived in 1847.

The Urban Scene

In a predominately rural area such as the Lake District, there are few towns. The major ones actually within the Lake District are Kendal (which has a separate chapter), Keswick and Windermere. Other towns on the fringe of the district include Cockermouth and Penrith. This section of photographs covers the urban aspect of the Lake District.

Keswick, The Bridge and Greta Hall 1889
22086
Here we see the bridge over the River Greta in the busy little market town of Keswick in the northern Lakes. In the distance, on the left of the picture, can just be seen Greta Hall, former home of the poets Samuel Taylor Coleridge and Robert Southey. The pencil works of A Banks on the right is an example of one of Keswick's major industries, founded on supplies of plumbago, or black lead, from the Seathwaite valley in Borrowdale.

▼ **Keswick, The Parish Church 1889** 22084
The elegant spire and pinnacles of the parish church of St John feature in many views of this town, situated at the foot of Skiddaw in the northern Lake District. The church was built in the 19th century on a slight hill, and also enjoys fine views over Derwent Water.

▼ **Windermere, Riggs Hotel 1929** 82820
Richard Rigg opened his Windermere Hotel in 1847 - the same year as the Kendal and Windermere Railway reached the town - and his yellow-and-black coaches provided a connecting service from the adjacent station to various parts of the Lake District. The hotel is now known as the Windermere Hotel.

▲ **Penrith, The Market Place 1893** 32923
Penrith received its first market charter in 1223, and it has continued as a busy market town serving the north-east of the Lake District and the North Pennines ever since. This view shows the Clock Tower and a surprisingly empty Market Place.

◄ **Bowness, The Promenade 1925** 77886
The provision of the public gardens of the Promenade at Bowness also followed the coming of the railway in 1847, and the increased popularity of the Lake District as a health-giving holiday resort for people from the industrial towns and cities of the north west.

Penrith, Cornmarket c1955 P33012
The Clock Tower which we saw in picture No 32923 can just be seen in the background. Horse-drawn transport is obviously still in use, but it is about to be phased out by the motorised vehicles which were taking over the streets of the Cumbrian town.

Penrith, King Street c1960 P33023
We are looking down Penrith's main shopping street. The scene has not changed much since Victorian days, except for the fact that the horses have by now disappeared and have been replaced by motor vehicles.

Penrith, The Parish Church 1893 32924
The square red sandstone west tower of St Andrew's Parish Church is Norman, and was part of the original church on the site. But the classical proportions of the rest of the church date from an extensive rebuilding in 1720. The whole building was restored by Sir A Richardson in 1945. The Saxon crosses of the Giant's Grave are in the churchyard (see the chapter on monuments and houses).

Cockermouth, General View 1906 54987
Cockermouth is situated where the River Cocker joins the River Derwent on its way to the Irish Sea at Workington. This view looks across the Workington to Cockermouth railway line, which opened in 1847, towards the spire of the parish church of All Saints on the right.

▲ **Cockermouth, Wordsworth's Birthplace c1955**
C133005
England's best known Romantic poet was born in this Georgian mansion in Cockermouth's Main Street in 1770. His father was steward to Sir James Lowther, and moved to the house in 1766. The house overlooks the River Derwent and has a delightful garden and terrace. It is now in the care of the National Trust.

◀ **Cockermouth, Main Street 1906** 54992
The clock tower dominates the main street of the West Cumberland town. Cockermouth was granted its market charter in 1221, and gradually developed in importance until it was the chief commercial centre of the old county of Cumberland.

Transport

The first tourists to the Lake District arrived by coach-and-four, and the most usual form of local transport was packhorse or horse and cart. By the time this collection of photographs were taken, the railway had arrived, but it was still to be many years before the Lakeland roads were to become choked with motor cars as they are today.

◄ **Windermere, The Ferry Boat 1896** 38802
The Bowness Ferry across the narrowest part of the lake was originally a hand-rowed operation. But in 1870, twenty-six years before this photograph was taken, it became steam-operated; this resulted in the building of the Ferry Hotel on the western shore in 1879. In this photograph, carts are being transported across the lake by the chain-operated pulley ferry.

▼ **Windermere, The Ferry Boat 1887** 20462

◄ **Bowness, The Boat Station and the Old England Hotel 1893**
31938
In the background is the Old England Hotel, one of many which sprang up in this little town as tourism took hold in the Lake District at the turn of the 19th century. The ivy-covered facade has not changed significantly.

Windermere, The Ferry Boat 1896 38800
Another view of the Bowness Ferry shows a full coach-and-four just about to set out from the Bowness side of the lake, with the ferry man James Coward at the front steadying the nervous horses. This must have been a special trip, because by this time the sight of a coach-and-four was becoming increasingly rare.

Windermere, Sailing Boats 1896 38804
Organised sailing on Windermere started in the mid 19th century. The Windermere Sailing Club, later to become the Royal Windermere Yacht Club, was founded in 1860, and organised regular regattas on the lake. This photograph shows a regatta in progress near Bowness-on-Windermere.

Windermere, Waterhead 1912 64319
Horse-drawn coaches wait patiently to take passengers from the boats at Waterhead, near Ambleside on Windermere. The ornate Waterhead buildings served an increasing trade of tourists to the area, particularly after the railway came in 1847.

▼ **Bowness, The Ferry arriving at the Nab c1955** B166017
By the time this photograph was taken, cars had replaced the horses and carts, and the crossing was accomplished by a chain-operated pulley. The wooded Claife Heights on the western shore are prominent in the background.

▼ **Ambleside, Waterhead Ferry 1912** 64321
A crowded WSV 'Tern' prepares to embark on a trip down Windermere from the Waterhead pier on a summer's day. The Edwardian costumes of the passengers are interesting to note - the ladies are all wearing the large hats and long dresses of the time, while most of the men sport straw hats or bowlers.

▲ **Bowness Pier, The Pleasure Steamer 'Teal' 1896** 38795
Packed to the gunwales, the newly-commissioned pleasure steamer 'Teal' leaves Bowness Pier for a trip on Windermere. At this time, private boat ownership was beyond the means of all but the wealthiest visitors, so this was most people's only chance of enjoying the scenery from the lake.

◄ **Newby Bridge, The River Leven 1914** 67412
Holidaymakers are boating on the southern reaches of Windermere near Newby Bridge. This is still a popular pastime on Windermere, which is England's largest lake; the calm reaches of the southern end of the lake provide a quiet backwater compared to the busy area around Bowness.

**Coniston, Waterhead
1912** 64281
Waterhead on Coniston
Water has not changed
significantly since this
photograph was taken.
Even the elegant steam
cruiser the 'Gondola',
seen here moored at
the pier, is still taking
passengers up and
down the lake.
Originally built in 1859,
it was rescued as a
rotting hulk and
restored to public use
by the National Trust in
1980.

◀ **Eskdale Green, The Ravenglass & Eskdale Railway c1950** E194071
The narrow-gauge Ravenglass & Eskdale Railway - affectionately known as 'Lil' Ratty' - opened in 1875, to link iron mines in Eskdale to the main line at Ravenglass. Restoration by a group of railway enthusiasts led to its reopening in 1960, and it is now a major tourist attraction. This view was taken near Eskdale in the 1950s.

Silecroft, The Railway Station c1950 S657018

Carlisle and Sons' delivery van waits at the level crossing near Silecroft Station on the west coast route between Barrow and Workington, which opened to traffic in 1848. Silecroft, near Millom, stands at the southernmost extremity of the Lake District National Park, at the foot of Black Combe (1,970 ft).

Newby Bridge, The Railway Station 1914
67417

A steam train pulls into Newby Bridge Station, at the southern end of Windermere. The Ulverston to Lakeside line was built in 1869, but closed and then reopened again in 1965 as a tourist railway, known as the Lakeside and Haverthwaite Railway.

Penrith, Hugh's Crag Bridge 1893 32943

Hugh's Crag Bridge is on the Penrith to Cockermouth line. The line was opened in 1864 to link the iron industry of West Cumberland with coal from the West Durham coalfield, but it soon became popular with tourists visiting Keswick and the northern Lake District.

Monuments
and Houses

Probably because of its remoteness and lack of development, the Lake District is well-blessed with ancient monuments, from prehistoric stone circles and standing stones to the ruins of medieval castles. In addition, when the district became fashionable during the 18th and 19th centuries, the landed gentry chose it to build some of their most extravagant stately homes.

Eamont Bridge, Mayburgh Henge 1893 32935

Castlerigg, The Druids' Circle 1895 36951
Erroneously known at the time when this photograph was taken as the Druids' Circle, the Castlerigg Stone Circle just outside Keswick is dramatically set in an amphitheatre of hills, including Skiddaw, seen in the background (left). It is thought to date from the Neolithic or early Bronze Age periods, predating the Druids by many centuries.

Shap, The Abbey 1893 32969
Shap Abbey, near the banks of the River Lowther, was founded by the 'white canons' of the Premonstratensian order at the end of the 12th century, but it was dissolved, like so many others, in 1540. This photograph shows the imposing west tower, which was built about 1500, and which still stands almost to its full height.

Kendal, The Castle 1894 34087
Kendal Castle was built by the Normans to the east of the town, probably by Ivo de Tailbois, the first Lord of Kendal in the late 12th century, and it still commands good views to the north and south-east. The castle was described as 'ready to drop down with age' by the beginning of the 17th century.

Kendal, The Castle 1896 38538
Katherine Parr, Henry VIII's sixth and surviving wife, was born here in 1512; at that time the castle was in the hands of Sir Thomas Parr. This view shows the exterior of the main hall, the most impressive part of the ruins, and now the centre of a public park.

Penrith, The Churchyard, The Giant's Grave 1893 32926
The so-called Giant's Grave in the churchyard of St Andrew's is actually a pair of tall Norse-influenced Saxon crosses with two hog-backed grave slabs in between. Legend has it that this is the grave of Ewan Caesario, a giant who was King of Cumbria.

Penrith, The Castle 1893 32928
Penrith Castle was built by William Strickland, later Bishop of Carlisle, who was given permission to build Penrith Castle in 1397, following the sacking of the town by raiding Scots in 1354. The curtain wall, shown in this photograph, is all that remains of Strickland's castle, which is now a public park.

Lowther Castle 1893 33514
This is not so much a castle, more a country house, built for the first Earl of Lonsdale by Sir Robert Smirke in 1806-11. The previous residence on the site dated from the 17th century, but had been badly damaged by fire in 1720. Lowther itself was gutted in 1957.

▼ **Holker Hall 1894** 34106
The west wing of the original old hall at Holker, home of the Preston family since the 16th century, was destroyed by fire in 1871. This sumptuous rebuilding, supervised by the seventh Duke of Devonshire, was designed by Paley and Austin of Lancaster, and has been described as their most outstanding domestic work.

▼ **Penrith, Eden Hall 1893** 32946
Here we see the colonnaded front and formal gardens of Eden Hall, four miles east of Penrith. Demolished in the 1930s, Eden Hall stood on the site of an earlier medieval house built by the Musgrave family. It was home to a legend concerning a 700-year-old glass cup: while it was kept complete, the cup would safeguard the future of the house.

▲ **Penrith, Brougham Castle 1893** 32938
The imposing red sandstone ruins of the keep of Brougham Castle watch over the River Eamont. Brougham Castle was originally built by the Normans, and was strengthened by Henry II in 1170. This was one of many castles to which Lady Anne Clifford, Countess of Dorset, made improvements, and she died here at the age of 90 in 1678.

◀ **Cockermouth, The Castle 1906** 55001
Cockermouth Castle was built in the 13th century on a strategic site to guard the confluence of the River Cocker and Derwent. Modifications, including a barbican and outer gatehouse, were made by Edward III in the 14th century, but the castle fell into ruin after a Civil War siege by Royalist forces in 1648.

Windermere, Wray Castle and the Boathouse 1886 18665
The stately Gothic pile of Wray Castle can just be seen peeping over the trees in the background of this
photograph, taken near its boathouse on the lake. Wray Castle was built by Dr James Dawson, a retired Liverpool
surgeon, between 1840-7, and is one of the most extravagant of the 19th-century Lake District mansions. It is now
a Merchant Navy training college.

Sizergh Castle 1896 38542
We are inside the three-sided courtyard of Sizergh Castle, near Kendal. Originally a 14th-century defensive pele
tower, Sizergh was the home of the Strickland family; the present building is mainly a 15th-century Elizabethan
mansion, now in the care of the National Trust.

Levens Hall, The Gardens 1891   28630
The magnificent topiary gardens of Levens Hall, near Kendal, were laid out by the King's gardener Beaumont, who trained at Versailles, in 1692. Levens Hall is a fine Elizabethan mansion built for the Bagot family around 1580, again around a 14th-century pele tower.

The Rural Scene

Outside the towns and villages of the Lake District, the rural scene had not changed much in many centuries. The small, isolated farmhouses and dalehead hamlets looked much as they had done since they were first established in the Middle Ages and before, as this selection of photographs shows.

Buttermere, Haymaking c1955 B260064
Agriculture in the 1950s had not changed much since the 19th century, and horses were still commonly used on the land. This scene, showing the loading of a hay wagon on the shores of Buttermere, with Honister Crag and Fleetwith Pike prominent in the background, demonstrates that timeless way of life.

Buttermere, The Village 1889 22055
The hamlet at the foot of Buttermere in the western Lake District takes its name from the lake; it is still the farming settlement it has always been. This view looks up the lake towards the skyline peaks of Fleetwith Pike on the left and Haystacks on the right.

Buttermere, High Stile 1889 22065
Buttermere takes its name from Old English, and means 'the lake by the dairy pastures' - where the butter is made. The farmstead of High Stile is still in the same business a thousand years later.

Buttermere, The Hotel c1873 6805
The hotel at Buttermere, formerly known as the Fish Hotel, was the scene in 1802 of a great scandal: the landlord's daughter, Mary Robinson or 'the Maid of Buttermere', married a man who claimed to be a gentleman, but who in fact was a fraudster. He was later hanged at Carlisle.

▼ **Buttermere, The Village 1889** 22057
The small stock enclosure which goes across the Sail Beck was probably used for sheep washing in the summer, before shearing.

▼ **Borrowdale, The Hotel 1895** 36947
The Borrowdale Hotel is in one of the wildest valleys of Lakeland. Early tourists were 'horrified' at the expanses of naked rock and impending mountains of places like Borrowdale, and feared to travel far into the dale, until poets like Wordsworth popularised the 'picturesque' mountain scenery.

▲ **Borrowdale, The Hotel 1870** 5047
This very early postcard view of the Borrowdale Hotel, with Grange Crags behind, shows the Lake District as it was before the tourist invasion really took hold. The traffic-free minor road meanders south between drystone walls through the dale, towards Grange and Rosthwaite.

◄ **Grange-in-Borrowdale, General View 1893** 32887
Grange is the hamlet at the foot of Borrowdale, where the River Derwent, seen on the left of this photograph, meanders through water meadows into mighty Derwent Water to the north. The name 'grange' signifies an outlying farm, usually belonging to a monastery.

Borrowdale, Grange 1893 32886
Grange-in-Borrowdale was originally founded as an outlying settlement from the medieval monastery of Furness Abbey. It is a popular centre for fell walkers. The peak of High Spy is in the background.

Wasdale Head, The Church 1889 22075
The tiny church of St Olaf at Wasdale Head is said to be among the smallest in England; but surrounded as it is by the dramatic mountains of Wasdale, it is also one of the most visited. There are many memorials in the 400-year-old building to walkers and climbers who have met their deaths on England's highest hills.

Wastwater, The Victoria Hotel 1889 22077
Wasdale and Wastwater can be said to have seen the birth of the sport of rock climbing, and climbers from all over Britain stayed at local hostelries such as the Victoria Hotel. Walter Haskett-Smith's first ascent of Napes Needle on Great Gable in 1886 - only three years before this photograph was taken - is widely held to be the advent of the sport.

Borrowdale, The Bowder Stone 1893 32891
The Bowder Stone, a 2,000-ton boulder which was transported to near Grange in Borrowdale by Ice Age glaciers, has been a source of tourist wonder for centuries. Today the stone is surrounded by trees; there is still a wooden staircase to reach the top.

Crummock Water, Scale Force 1893 32914
Scale Force near Crummock Water is, at 172 ft, the Lake District's longest waterfall. The path to the falls goes up from Buttermere village; the falls - in fact a series of cascades - are hidden in a tree-lined gorge.

Langdale, Dungeon Ghyll Force 1888 20499
These dramatic falls are hidden in the depths of Dungeon Ghyll in Great Langdale, and are seldom visited by car-bound tourists. The falls are caused by the waters of the Dungeon Ghyll, which rises on the Langdale Pikes above, and crashes through this tiny gorge of sheer-sided rocks.

Ambleside, The Stepping Stones 1888
20484
A crinoline-clad Victorian lady delicately picks her way across the stepping stones which cross the River Rothay, near Ambleside. Ladies were not seen in walking trousers or breeches in those days!

Ambleside, Sweden Bridge 1912 64330d
High Sweden Bridge is a picturesque packhorse bridge over the Scandale Beck between High Pike and Snarker Pike (there is a Low Sweden Bridge lower down the valley). It has no direct Scandinavian connection, other than the fact that the name comes from the Norse 'svithinn', which means 'land cleared by burning'.

Ambleside, Tarn Hows c1955 A46145
This is a classic view of Tarn Hows, near Hawkshead, with the peaks of the Langdale Pikes in the centre background. Despite its natural appearance, the lakes of Tarn Hows are in fact artificial, and there were once several smaller tarns. About 80 years ago, the landowner dammed the beck to create this familiar scene - one of the most visited places in the Lake District.

Ambleside, Stock Ghyll Force 1886 18686
The waterfalls of Stock Ghyll Force have been a major attraction to visitors to Ambleside for well over a century; this is a very early photograph of them. The waters of Stock Ghyll rise just below the summit of the Kirkstone Pass, north of the town, and plunge through this wooded gorge before joining the River Rothay and eventually entering Windermere.

Greenodd, The Leven Estuary 1921 70699
Greenodd stands on the Leven Estuary where the River Leven from Windermere and the River Crake from Coniston Water flow into Morecambe Bay and the Irish Sea. The line of the Furness Railway, built in 1857, can be seen crossing the bay on the embankment to the right.

The Lakes

It is the lakes which give the Lake District its name, and they are what brings the majority of the tourists to the area. But there are several common misconceptions about them. There are actually only 16 lakes in the Lake District - and only one, Bassenthwaite, is actually called a lake. All the rest are 'meres' or 'waters', while the smaller mountain lakes are known as 'tarns'; they were all originally formed in troughs gouged out by Ice Age glaciers.

Windermere, The Ferry Boat 1887 20461
This is the original hand-rowed ferry service across the narrowest part of the Windermere at Bowness Nab. The lady in her long black dress and the gentleman wait for the ferryman to take them across to the western side of the lake, where the wooded Claife Heights stretch away to the right.

◄ **Windermere 1912**
64311
We are looking south down the length of Windermere from Todd Crag, a southern outlier of Loughrigg Fell above the hamlet of Clappersgate. Immediately below the viewpoint, the River Rothay winds into England's largest lake by Gale Naze Crag in the centre of the picture.

Windermere, From Biskey How 1887 20438
The newly-built villas of Bowness-on-Windermere spread out towards the viewpoint of Biskey How in this view of the lake, looking towards the wooded island of Belle Isle, with the Claife Heights beyond.

Windermere, The Nickle Landing Stage 1914 67419
A small boy in a rowing boat gazes at his reflection in the waters of Windermere in this summer photograph. The location is the Nickle Landing Stage, near Newby Bridge, at the southern end of the lake, where it narrows to enter the River Leven.

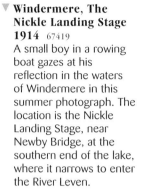

Windermere, Ambleside, Waterside 1912 64316
A long line of rowing boats waiting for their customers stretch around the bay at Waterhead, near Ambleside. In the distance, Todd Crag and Loughrigg Fell fill in the left background.

Windermere, The Waterhead Hotel 1887 20463
Another view of Waterhead shows the Waterhead Hotel, built to serve the increasing numbers of tourists who were arriving by train at the lakeside station at Bowness, and catching a steamer up the lake to Waterhead.

Windermere, A Distant View 1886 18663
In this tranquil scene, a farmer rests on a fence overlooking Windermere. The wooden gates and fences in the photograph are typical of this southern, less-mountainous part of the Lake District, and the slightly-blurred leaves of the silver birch trees are caused by wind movement.

Buttermere, By the Lake 1893 32903
These elegant Scots pines on the shores of Buttermere are among the most photographed of any in the Lake District, but this must be one of the earliest pictures of them. The fells in the background are High Crag and High Stile, with Comb Crags and Burtness Combe in between.

Buttermere, General View 1893 32896
This photograph was taken from Gatesgarth with Whiteless Pike in the background. Gatesgarth is a place name which comes from Old Norse language, as do many in the higher hills of the Lake District. It means 'the pass where the goats go'.

Buttermere, General View 1889 22052
We are looking north from Lower Gatesgarth. The pines of Crag Wood are prominent in the centre of the photograph, while the slopes of Dodd sweep up the lake shore beyond. Buttermere and Crummock Water were once one large lake, until alluvium from Sail Beck gradually cut it in two.

◄ **Derwent Water and
Skiddaw, From
Ashness Bridge 1893**
32870
Seen on countless
calendars, this view of
Derwent Water from
Ashness Bridge, on the
narrow road up to
Watendlath, is always
popular. Skiddaw fills the
backdrop. Cat Gill is the
stream which plunges
under the bridge on its
way down to meet
Derwent Water.

Esthwaite Water, Roger Ground from Colthouse Heights 1912 64290
An Edwardian lady relaxes in a meadow on Colthouse Heights, on the eastern shores of Esthwaite Water, looking across to the knoll of Roger Ground, near Hawkshead. Esthwaite Water, south of Hawkshead, is one of the quietest of the lakes, and is a Norse name meaning 'the lake by the eastern clearing'.

Crummock Water, From Ling Crag c1893 32912
Whiteless Pike (2,159 ft) is the prominent fell in this view, which was taken from Crummock Water below Mellbreak, with Rannerdale Knotts on the right of the photograph. This view is virtually unchanged today.

Keswick and Derwent Water, From Latrigg 1889 22079
The isolated outlier of Latrigg (1,203 ft) is an easy stroll from Keswick; it gives a grandstand view of the 'capital' of the northern Lakes. The wooded islands of Derwent, Lord's and St Herbert's are clearly visible, as are the background Newlands Fells.

Crummock Water, From Loweswater 1889 22139
A picnic party in a meadow in the hamlet of Loweswater are enjoying the splendid view north up Crummock Water. The lower slopes of Grasmoor are prominent on the left, and the skyline is filled by Fleetwith Pike, Haystacks and High Crag. Rannerdale Knotts is the small dark hill in the middle distance above the lake.

Derwent Water, The Ruskin Monument, Friar's Crag 1906 54984
This simple stone obelisk on the summit of Friar's Crag, Derwent Water, commemorates the great Victorian critic and Lake District conservationist John Ruskin, whose early memory was apparently being taken by his nurse to this spot.

Derwent Water, Friar's Crag and Causey Pike 1906 54982
This is another of the Lake District's classic viewpoints, the backdrop formed by the peak of Causey Pike (2,035 ft). Friar's Crag is thought to have got its name as the embarkation point from monks visiting St Herbert on his island in the lake.

Derwent Water, The Lodore Hotel 1893 32878
The Lodore Hotel, at the southern end of Derwent Water, is a fine Victorian Gothic structure, built at the foot of the twin cascades known as the Lodore Falls, which were very popular in the Victorian era. The crag in the background of this picture is Shepherd's Crag, a popular venue for rock climbers today.

▼ **Thirlmere, From Hell How 1892** 30562
This is an historic photograph of Thirlmere, taken from Hell How. It shows the last
of the original two lakes - Leathe's Water and Wythburn Water - which formerly
filled the valley below Helvellyn; they were joined and became the Thirlmere
Reservoir when Manchester Corporation built the four-mile long reservoir between
1890-2.

▼ **Thirlmere, General View 1888** 20554
This view shows the northern end of Thirlmere, looking towards Great
How Wood and the Castle Rock of Triermain. Note the young conifers,
recently planted in the interest of water purity, which now cloak the
artificial lake with their dense canopy of branches.

▲ **Wastwater, The Lake
1889** 22067
This is one of the classic
views of the Lake District;
it is now used by the
modern National Park
Authority as its logo. This
photograph of the
northern shore of
Wastwater shows (left to
right) the trio of peaks at
the head of England's
deepest lake - Yewbarrow
(2,061 ft), Great Gable
(2,949 ft) and Lingmell
(2,649 ft).

◄ **Ullswater, From Place Fell 1892** 30548
Ullswater snakes into the Lake District hills for seven and a half miles, from Pooley Bridge to Glenridding, and has three major and quite different stretches. This view, looking west from the slopes of Place Fell, is towards the head of the lake at Glenridding, and shows the northern stretch.

Rydal Water, General View 1886 18691
We are on the peaceful, reed-fringed shores of Rydal Water, near Grasmere. Rydal was the home of William Wordsworth from 1813 until his death in 1850, and this was one of his favourite lakes. This well-wooded little lake is now in the hands of the National Trust.

Wastwater, On the Shore 1889 22110
This tranquil scene shows a rowing boat moored on the northern shore of Wastwater. The trees of Low Wood stretch out into the lake, while the steep scree-clad slopes of Illgill Head - the famous Wasdale Screes - soar up the southern shores.

Kendal

Kendal -the 'Auld Grey Town' on the River Kent - was founded on the wealth won from the wool of Lakeland sheep. Its motto is 'Pannis mihi Panis', which means 'wool is my bread'; even Shakespeare refers to Kendal Green cloth in Henry IV Part 1. But wool was not Kendal's only industry, and many other trades set themselves up in the many yards which lead off the main street of this southern gateway to the Lakes.

Kendal, Stricklandgate 1888 21088
Stricklandgate, the northern extension of Highgate, is one of Kendal's main thoroughfares. The name means 'the road leading to the stirk land', and was often referred to as the Drover's Road, where cattle were driven from the north. This view, looking north, shows a traffic-free street.

Kendal, General View 1896 38526
This is a general view of Kendal from the south, with the Lakeland hills in the background. The town of Kendal was founded on the west bank of the River Kent, although the earliest settlement around the castle was on the east bank.

Kendal, The Market 1924 75795
Kendal was granted the right to hold a market as early as 1189, when it was also made a barony. The Market Place had been enclosed on four sides until 1909, when it was opened to Stricklandgate, from where this view was taken. It shows the newly unveiled war memorial in the foreground.

Kendal, An Old Yard off Stricklandgate 1914 67398
One of the most engaging characteristics of Kendal is its multitude of charming side alleys and yards, such as this
one off the main thoroughfare of Stricklandgate.

Kendal, Stramongate Bridge 1896 38527
Miller Bridge, once known as Mill Bridge because it linked the mills on the east of the river with the town, is one of the chief bridges across the River Kent. This view shows the twin spires of the Roman Catholic church beyond.

Kendal, Nether Bridge 1914 67381
Here we see the lower or Nether Bridge across the River Kent. Now part of the one-way system, the Nether Bridge links the older, western side of Kendal with the newer, eastern suburbs.

Kendal, Collin Croft 1914 67384
This imposing archway led up a flight of steps to another of Kendal's famous yards; this one lies off the main street, Highgate. The use of the word 'gate', meaning a road or street, comes from the Old Norse 'gata', and is another clue to the antiquity of the town.

Kendal, The Grammar School 1896 38530
Kendal Grammar School sits alongside the banks of the River Kent. Ten years before this photograph was taken, the school had amalgamated with the famous old Blue Coat School, which had itself been founded in 1670 to prepare boys for the Grammar School.

Kendal, Highgate 1914 67393
A lad sits on his handcart on the right of this photograph, taken in a yard off Highgate. He appears to be in conversation with a friend seated on the other side of the cobbled yard, while others look on as they pose for the camera.

Kendal, Stramongate 1914 67387
This yard, complete with children posed on the steps in the centre, led off Stramongate, the main approach to Kendal from the north-east, from Penrith or Appleby. Stramongate means 'the street of the straw men', presumably those who brought the straw to the cattle market.

Kendal, The County Hotel 1924 75801
The County Hotel is one of the main hotels in the centre of Kendal; it dominates this part of the old town, whose wealth was founded on the woollen and textile industries. The famed Kendal bowmen at the Battle of Flodden Field (1513) were clad in home-spun Kendal Green cloth.

Kendal, The New Shambles 1914 67400
The New Shambles, off Finkle Street, was built in 1803. The word 'shambles' comes from the Old English 'sceamol', which originally meant a bench for the sale of meat. The New Shambles replaced the Old Shambles, which was on the west side of Highgate. As we can see in this photograph, many types of shop occupied the units in the New Shambles.

Kendal, Rainbow Hotel Yard 1914 67389
The old coaching inn known as the Rainbow was one of the many which had run back from Kendal's main streets since the Middle Ages. The cobbled yard and upper floor gallery are typical of a coaching inn, and once echoed to the sound of horses' hooves as they dashed in through the narrow archway.

Kendal, An Old Gateway 1914 67385
The datestone above this old archway gives its age as 1659. During the 17th century, Kendal expanded rapidly as a market town serving the southern part of the Lake District, and this gateway was one of many which served the yards where the woollen merchants plied their trade.

Kendal, Branthwaite Brow 1914 67383
Branthwaite Brow is one of the three streets which meet Kent Street as it leads up the steep hill opposite Miller Bridge. The others are Finkle Street and Stramongate. This view looks down Branthwaite Brow towards the River Kent.

The Fells and Passes

The earliest tourists to the Lake District were overwhelmed by the 'horrid' and 'frightful' nature of the mountains and crags, which frowned down on them as they negotiated the passes. It was Wordsworth and the other Romantic poets who first instilled the idea that the Lakeland fells had their own beauty and attractions, as generations of walkers and climbers have found since.

◄ **Borrowdale, Seathwaite, Stockley Bridge 1889**
22017
Grains Gill tumbles over a series of cascades beneath Stockley Bridge, near Seathwaite in Borrowdale, with Aaron Crags prominent on Seathwaite Fell in the background. The view is hardly changed today.

▼ **Keswick, Skiddaw 1889** 22089
Snow dusts the shapely 3,053 ft summit of Skiddaw, the giant among the northern fells, and one of the first popular mountain climbs in the Lake District. This winter view was taken from St John's-in-the-Vale, and also shows Lonscale Fell to the right.

Helvellyn, Striding Edge 1912 64342
This is one of the classic mountain views in the Lake District, with the glaciated knife-edge of Striding Edge leading off eastwards towards High Spying How from the 3,118 ft summit of Helvellyn, one of the most popular mountains in the Lake District. It is interesting that this view clearly shows the footpath along the edge, which was obviously being well used even then.

Honister Pass and Honister Crag 1889 22015
The great eastern face of Honister Crag dominates the Honister Pass between Borrowdale and Buttermere and Crummock Water, which can be seen in the distance. The Gatesgarthdale Beck flows through the valley. To the left can be seen the workings of the Honister Slate Quarry, which produced some of the finest-quality green slate roofing and walling.

Kirkstone Pass 1886 5010
Francis Frith's coachman takes a well-earned rest. His carriage has stopped near the summit of one of the most famous of the Lake District passes. It connects Troutbeck with Patterdale. The pass is said to have taken its name from a large rock which looks like a gable end of a church. This view looks south towards Troutbeck, with the shoulder of Broad End on the left.

Great End 1889 22024
This view of Great Gable is unusual, as it is taken from the north. The usual view of the shapeliest mountains in the Lake District is from the head of Wasdale, where it dominates the scene. The 2,949 ft summit has a tablet in memory of the members of the Fell and Rock Climbing Club who died in the First World War. It was unveiled when the mountain was handed over to the National Trust.

Langdale Pike 1892 30518
The Langdale Pikes are among the Lake District's most popular and recognisable hills. This view was taken from near the Dungeon Ghyll Hotel in Great Langdale, a popular starting point for walking the hills. Stickle Ghyll, which flows down from Stickle Tarn, passes under the bridge in this view, which looks towards the 2,403 ft summit of Harrison Stickle, the highest of the pikes.

Ennerdale, From Green Gable 1889 22018
This view looks north-west down Ennerdale from Great Gable's sister peak, Green Gable. Much of this lovely valley is now cloaked under a blanket of conifers, as are so many of the Lake District dales. The Black Sail Youth Hostel near the head of Ennerdale is one of the most remote in Britain.

Grasmere Vale 1926 79213
There is not much traffic - a car and a motorcycle with pillion passenger - in this view of the road running down from Dunmail Raise into Grasmere. The lake and village of Grasmere can be seen in the distance, while to the right, the 'Lion and Lamb' summit rocks of Helm Crag are seen silhouetted against the skyline.

Coniston, The Fells 1912 64276
A horse and cart wends its way up a gated minor road through the Coniston Fells. At the time before the coming of the motor car in significant numbers, there were many roads like this in the Lake District, and life continued among the hills at the same leisurely pace as it had for centuries.

Little Langdale 1888 20495
This view from Little Langdale looks towards Langdale Pikes, with the thimble-shaped Pike 'o' Stickle (2,323 ft) prominent on the left, and Gimmer Crag, and Harrison Stickle (2,403 ft) on the right in the distance. The slopes of Blake Rigg rise towards the left of the photograph.

Great Langdale 1888 20497
Pike 'o' Stickle (2,323 ft) is the thimble-shaped peak prominent on the skyline in this view taken from near the head of Great Langdale. In the scree slope just visible below the summit of Pike 'o' Stickle, a prehistoric axe factory was discovered: here, the hard volcanic tuff was shaped into axes and transported all over Britain.

Index

The Francis Frith Collection publishes over 100 new titles each year. A selection of those currently available is listed below. For latest catalogue please contact The Francis Frith Collection.
Town Books 96 pages, approximately 75 photos. **County and Themed Books** 128 pages, approximately 135 photos (unless specified). Pocket Albums are miniature editions of Frith local history books 128 pages, approximately 95 photos.

Available from your local bookshop or from the publisher

Lancaster, Morecambe and Heysham Pocket Album
Leeds Pocket Album
Leicester
Leicestershire
Lincolnshire Living Memoires
Lincolnshire Pocket Album
Liverpool and Merseyside
London Pocket Album
Ludlow
Maidenhead
Maidstone
Malmesbury
Manchester Pocket Album
Marlborough
Matlock
Merseyside Living Memories
Nantwich and Crewe
New Forest
Newbury Living Memories
Newquay to St Ives
North Devon Living Memories
North London
North Wales
North Yorkshire
Northamptonshire
Northumberland
Northwich
Nottingham
Nottinghamshire Pocket Album
Oakham
Odiham Then and Now
Oxford Pocket Album
Oxfordshire
Padstow
Pembrokeshire
Penzance
Petersfield Then and Now
Plymouth
Poole and Sandbanks
Preston Pocket Album
Ramsgate Old and New
Reading Pocket Album
Redditch Living Memories
Redhill to Reigate
Richmond
Ringwood
Rochdale
Romford Pocket Album
Salisbury Pocket Album
Scotland
Scottish Castles
Sevenoaks and Tonbridge
Sheffield and South Yorkshire Pocket Album
Shropshire
Somerset
South Devon Coast
South Devon Living Memories
South East London

Southampton Pocket Album
Southend Pocket Album
Southport
Southwold to Aldeburgh
Stourbridge Living Memories
Stratford upon Avon
Stroud
Suffolk
Suffolk Pocket Album
Surrey Living Memories
Sussex
Sutton
Swanage and Purbeck
Swansea Pocket Album
Swindon Living Memories
Taunton
Teignmouth
Tenby and Saundersfoot
Tiverton
Torbay
Truro
Uppingham
Villages of Kent
Villages of Surrey
Villages of Sussex Pocket Album
Wakefield and the Five Towns Living Memories
Warrington
Warwick
Warwickshire Pocket Album
Wellingborough Living Memories
Wells
Welsh Castles
West Midlands Pocket Album
West Wiltshire Towns
West Yorkshire
Weston-super-Mare
Weymouth
Widnes and Runcorn
Wiltshire Churches
Wiltshire Living Memories
Wiltshire Pocket Album
Wimborne
Winchester Pocket Album
Windermere
Windsor
Wirral
Wokingham and Bracknell
Woodbridge
Worcester
Worcestershire
Worcestershire Living Memories
Wyre Forest
York Pocket Album
Yorkshire
Yorkshire Coastal Memories
Yorkshire Dales
Yorkshire Revisited

See Frith books on the internet at www.francisfrith.com

FRITH PRODUCTS & SERVICES

Francis Frith would doubtless be pleased to know that the pioneering publishing venture he started in 1860 still continues today. Over a hundred and forty years later, The Francis Frith Collection continues in the same innovative tradition and is now one of the foremost publishers of vintage photographs in the world. Some of the current activities include:

INTERIOR DECORATION

Today Frith's photographs can be seen framed and as giant wall murals in thousands of pubs, restaurants, hotels, banks, retail stores and other public buildings throughout the country. In every case they enhance the unique local atmosphere of the places they depict and provide reminders of gentler days in an increasingly busy and frenetic world.

PRODUCT PROMOTIONS

Frith products are used by many major companies to promote the sales of their own products or to reinforce their own history and heritage. Frith promotions have been used by Hovis bread, Courage beers, Scots Porage Oats, Colman's mustard, Cadbury's foods, Mellow Birds coffee, Dunhill pipe tobacco, Guinness, and Bulmer's Cider.

GENEALOGY AND FAMILY HISTORY

As the interest in family history and roots grows world-wide, more and more people are turning to Frith's photographs of Great Britain for images of the towns, villages and streets where their ancestors lived; and, of course, photographs of the churches and chapels where their ancestors were christened, married and buried are an essential part of every genealogy tree and family album.

FRITH PRODUCTS

All Frith photographs are available Framed or just as Mounted Prints and Posters (size 23 x 16 inches). These may be ordered from the address below. Other products available are- Address Books, Calendars, Jigsaws, Canvas Prints, Notelets and local and prestige books.

THE INTERNET

Already ninety thousand Frith photographs can be viewed and purchased on the internet through the Frith websites and a myriad of partner sites.

For more detailed information on Frith companies and products, look at this site:
www.francisfrith.com

See the complete list of Frith Books at: www.francisfrith.com
This web site is regularly updated with the latest list of publications from The Francis Frith Collection. If you wish to buy books relating to another part of the country that your local bookshop does not stock, you may purchase on-line.

For further information, trade, or author enquiries please contact us at the address below:
The Francis Frith Collection, Unit 6, Oakley Business Park, Wylye Road, Dinton, Wiltshire SP3 5EU.
Tel: +44 (0)1722 716 376 Fax: +44 (0)1722 716 881 Email: sales@francisfrith.co.uk

See Frith products on the internet at www.francisfrith.com

FREE PRINT OF YOUR CHOICE

Mounted Print
Overall size 14 x 11 inches (355 x 280mm)

Choose any Frith photograph in this book.
Simply complete the Voucher opposite and return it with your remittance for £3.50 (to cover postage and handling) and we will print the photograph of your choice in SEPIA (size 11 x 8 inches) and supply it in a cream mount with a burgundy rule line (overall size 14 x 11 inches).
Please note: aerial photographs and photographs with a reference number starting with a "Z" are not Frith photographs and cannot be supplied under this offer. Offer valid for delivery to one UK address only.

PLUS: Order additional Mounted Prints at HALF PRICE - £9.50 each (normally £19.00)
If you would like to order more Frith prints from this book, possibly as gifts for friends and family, you can buy them at half price (with no additional postage and handling costs).

PLUS: Have your Mounted Prints framed
For an extra £18.00 per print you can have your mounted print(s) framed in an elegant polished wood and gilt moulding, overall size 16 x 13 inches (no additional postage and handling required).

IMPORTANT!

These special prices are only available if you use this form to order. You must use the ORIGINAL VOUCHER on this page (no copies permitted). We can only despatch to one UK address. This offer cannot be combined with any other offer.

Send completed Voucher form to:
The Francis Frith Collection, Unit 6, Oakley Business Park, Wylye Road, Dinton, Wiltshire SP3 5EU

CHOOSE A PHOTOGRAPH FROM THIS BOOK

 *for **FREE** and Reduced Price Frith Prints*

Please do not photocopy this voucher. Only the original is valid, so please fill it in, cut it out and return it to us with your order.

Picture ref no	Page no	Qty	Mounted @ £9.50	Framed + £18.00	Total Cost £
		1	Free of charge*	£	£
			£9.50	£	£
			£9.50	£	£
			£9.50	£	£
			£9.50	£	£
			£9.50	£	£

Please allow 28 days for delivery.
Offer available to one UK address only

* Post & handling		£3.50
Total Order Cost		**£**

Title of this book . . . .

I enclose a cheque/postal order for £ . . . .
made payable to 'The Francis Frith Collection'

OR please debit my Mastercard / Visa / Maestro card, details below

Card Number:

Issue No (Maestro only):   Valid from (Maestro):

Card Security Number: Expires:

Signature:

Name Mr/Mrs/Ms . . . .

Address . . . .

. . . .

. . . .

. . . . Postcode . . . .

Daytime Tel No . . . .

Email . . . .

978-1-85937-275-9   Valid to 31/12/14

Can you help us with information about any of the Frith photographs in this book?

We are gradually compiling an historical record for each of the photographs in the Frith archive. It is always fascinating to find out the names of the people shown in the pictures, as well as insights into the shops, buildings and other features depicted.

If you recognize anyone in the photographs in this book, or if you have information not already included in the author's caption, do let us know. We would love to hear from you, and will try to publish it in future books or articles.

An Invitation from The Francis Frith Collection to Share Your Memories

The 'Share Your Memories' feature of our website allows members of the public to add personal memories relating to the places featured in our photographs, or comment on others already added. Seeing a place from your past can rekindle forgotten or long held memories. Why not visit the website, find photographs of places you know well and add YOUR story for others to read and enjoy? We would love to hear from you!

www.francisfrith.com/memories

Our production team

Frith books are produced by a small dedicated team at offices near Salisbury. Most have worked with the Frith Collection for many years. All have in common one quality: they have a passion for the Frith Collection.

Frith Books and Gifts

We have a wide range of books and gifts available on our website utilising our photographic archive, many of which can be individually personalised.

www.francisfrith.com